BETWEEN THESE BONES

A COLLECTION OF POETRY

FREYA SHARP

BETWEEN THESE BONES

ISBN: 978-1-963705-88-1

Published in the United States of America by Harbor Lane Books, LLC.

www.harborlanebooks.com

This one is for me and maybe you, too.

all the things that happened to me
came without warning
so why do i need to warn you of the things you're about to read?

- life doesn't come with trigger warnings

the water doesn't get hot enough
to wash away the marks you left inside me
they said i suffered from third-degree burns
but they don't know what suffering means

at thirteen i was still playing with dolls
at fourteen i'd never even kissed a boy
at fifteen my innocence was stolen away
but why would they believe me
i loved him
and he loved me
i think
wait, no
shhh...
he whispered against my ear
i love you
he thought i wanted to hear
wait
my stomach dropped
stop
my heart raced
my mind couldn't catch up
i don't know
my voice cracked
but i...
shhh...it's okay
sometimes i can still hear the zipper sliding down
on his jean shorts
and the soft rumple that they made
when they hit his cream-colored carpeted floor
you love me?
my voice shook his bedroom window
love
i repeated it over and over in my head
i can't
his callused hands scraped across my legs
spreading them apart

no matter how hard i tried to squeeze them shut
he wasn't giving up
please stop
tears streamed down my face
shhh...it'll be okay
i'd never seen a penis before
only an illustration of one
i'd seen in a sex ed video in the fifth grade
the orange-red walls in his bedroom
pulled me away
from the nightmare i couldn't awake
they reminded me of a sunny place
those fucking walls were my saving grace

can you hear my silent screams?
my eyes will tell you things
my lips
teeth
and tongue
will never allow me to speak

i'll never forget the way your fists put me in my place day
after day
or the way your words shot through my chest like bullets
every chance you could take
i'll never forget the way your pocketknife slowly slid
between my ribs after the little snap
of breaking my porcelain skin
or the time you put that same knife to my throat as you
laughed and said it was just a joke
i'll never forget the smile on your face as you applauded my
tolerance for pain as blood streamed down my face
i'll never forget the feeling of being slammed against your
concrete floor
or the deafening sound of your screaming as you swore
you'd always love me more.
i'll never forget pissing my pants and puking all over your
couch after you choked me until i blacked out
i'll never forget the way you held me and ran your fingers
through my hair after pushing me down your basement
stairs
and the way you whispered that everything would be okay
because you'd always be there
i'll never forget the promises you made
every promise was always the same
you promised
and promised
things would change

- they didn't, but i did

i chose to keep quiet
in hopes that he would change
i chose to stay
and for those choices i paid
it's my fault i'm broke

- forever indebted to myself

you cannot drown your sorrows
in whiskey or gin
they may silence
but in the morning
they will breathe again

- *wishful drinking*

even if it's false
you're giving me hope
that's what gets me through
I need this
I need hope
I need you

he caught my breath
in the crack between his lips
and he ripped it from my lungs
without mercy.

- *i should have known better*

dismantle my being
it's okay
i want you to break me down
in the worst of ways
i want to feel your grip
the hatred in your palms
as you shred me apart
from head to toe
from heart to soul
i want to see
how ugly you can be
i want you to look me in the eyes
as you dismantle me
i just need to know
how bad you can make me hurt

you should have left my lips alone
i should have left my heart at home
you should have known better
i never wanted to fall for you
i only wanted to walk with you

i'm tired of leaving the light on every night
and listening to it whisper
you know he's not coming home, when will you ever learn?
do you think i turn it off, even though i know it's right?
no, i keep that damn light on in hopes that you'll sneak into
bed and lay your head upon my chest
you'll whisper
i love you, i'm so sorry
and i'll kiss your forehead and tell you
i need to sleep
because i'm so tired
mentally and physically drained
and you can finally see it
so, you'll lift your head and smile down upon me as you
watch me fall back to sleep
then a little tear will fall from your eye
and drip down your cheek as you wish me sweet dreams
then you'll fall asleep right next to me

aren't you exhausted?
i can see the lies packed in the bags under your eyes
don't you get tired of trying to remember if you're forgetting
anything?

it fascinates me
how words can dig so deep
sometimes
i say things
just to get under your skin.

i'm caught between loving him
and all of his broken parts
and leaving him and being free
but maybe i can fix him
maybe he can even fix me

- *toxicity*

i bare my bones to you
to break them as you please
to suck the marrow from them
and then leave

- *a glutton for punishment*

you are the dark
that drinks my light

- a thirst that cannot be quenched

she misses herself
the person she used to be
before he broke her

that piercing stare you give in frustration while pleading
your fidelity to me
i'd think you know by now
those lying eyes can no longer hide from me

piece by piece
i crumble to the floor
and wait for you
to sweep me up
and throw me away
like you always do

- *one man's trash is another man's treasure*

i
find
comfort
in
the
gentle
way
you
word
your
lies
as
you
whisper
them
to
me
every
night

life is all about
the little things
i think that's why
i'm content being spare change
because every piece of me
you toss to the side adds up
and one day you'll need me
one day i'll be worth enough

when you find a bobby pin on your floor
do you wonder if it's mine or hers?
do the memories flood your brain
of when i'd go insane
because i'd lose those damn things everywhere
and i had nothing to pin up my sex hair?
does she do the same thing?
i bet it drives you fucking crazy
when you find those damn bobby pins
all over your floor

he doesn't love you.
you're creating your own hell
and all he loves is watching you burn.

- *burning alive*

everything i hate in you
is everything i hate in me
everything you hate in me
is everything you hate in you
maybe one day you'll love you
and maybe one day i'll love me

- one can only hope

these cold empty sheets
keep getting the best of me
i lay here alone
and blame myself for your infidelities
but was it all me?
all i ever wanted was to make you happy
but i'm not her
and i never will be
was i too goofy to be sexy
was i too passionate and too deep
maybe you're just too shallow for me
i'm know one day when you're sleeping next to her
you'll be dreaming of me

sitting and sipping on this hot cup of coffee
replaying all the things that have happened
between you and me
and i honestly don't think
i could ever forgive you
for all the things i heard you say
when you thought i wasn't listening

i've never been enough
you always beg for more
i fill your cup
until it overflows
but mine is running low
they say you can't pour from a cup that's empty

- *please refill me*

it's amazing how blinding love can be
we brush all the dirty secrets beneath the rug
and we create something pretty
out of less than mediocrity
just for others to see
we forgive the unforgivable
and turn our cheeks
we promise ourselves
it won't happen anymore
but here we are yet again

- *what is the definition of insanity?*

swim a thousand miles
just to reach the depths of you
i am out of breath

- he said as he packed his things

i never knew our clock ticked
until you left
it taunts me every second
you're not here

- *it's always louder at night*

the easiest thing a man can do is walk away
from a woman who bends herself until she nearly breaks
just to keep a smile on his face
and the hardest thing a man will ever do is see the same
woman rise from the ashes he left her in
in that moment is when he'll realize
she never needed him
but he needs her

i'll always hear the words you never left unsaid
the ones where you said
you'd be better off dead
i get weak and start to think
that maybe just maybe
you were right
then i weep myself to sleep
and forget by morning rise
rinse and repeat
it's a never-ending battle
this grudge is eating me alive

imagine how dull life would be
if we never felt pain
just think about it
we all have a dark side
and we all love to play in the rain

you didn't break my heart
i'm not fragile
i don't need to be handled with care
you only saw a thread sticking out one day
and you tugged on it
slowly
day after day
completely unraveling it
and as soon as you saw the mess it made
you told me i should learn how to sew

you still linger
in my mouth
like the aftertaste
of burnt toast

time has snuck up and thrown me in a chokehold
memories flash before my eyes
it seems as though it all happened yesterday
but it's been years since i've seen your face
yet i can still taste the bitterness of your lips
the years may have passed,
but the memories stay.
and oh
those fucking nightmares
no
they don't go away
i suppose it's time for me to say
i forgive you,
but i'll never forget.
i forgive you,
but i'll never forget.

- if you tell a lie enough, it becomes the truth. isn't that what they say?

love stains can be washed out of these sheets
but not the memories.

i think about it all the time
what it would be like
to see your face again
to hear your voice
i wonder what you'd say
or if you'd say anything at all
because i always think about what i'd say
and i practice my lines almost everyday

- just in case you say you're sorry

i saw you standing there
smoking a cigarette

inhaling a memory
exhaling regret

she didn't want to be his whole world
she only wanted the two of them to exist in the same one

- *he's got her in the palm of his hands and he doesn't even know it*

if there were ever a time her love wasn't loud and clear
you weren't listening
for every kiss
every touch
every look
was deafening

- it costs nothing to pay attention

fleeting breaths
second guesses
half steps
forward and back
hesitation at its best
burrowing
softly, softly
into the marrow of my bones
making itself at home

- *anxiety-ridden*

it's not failure she fears
it's success
she's used to being last
or barely second best

i earned each of my thorns
and if they make you bleed
i have no reason to be sorry
it means you're much too close to me
take a step back
let me breathe
let me blossom peacefully

it wasn't until i was without you
i learned how to breathe again
and every now and then i find myself
missing the way you used to take my breath away

i need you to know
i forgive you
and all i can hope
is that you forgive me too

i miss the click of your cuffs
around my wrists
and the feel of the burn
as i'd fight against your bedpost

the wind wraps its fingers in my hair
just like you used to do

- *i miss you, feel free to send more signs*

he knows he has a skeleton key
and even if she locks all the doors
he can always get back in

they say you should pick your battles
but i don't know what to choose
between my head and my heart

- forever caught in the crossfire

when you feel the sadness lingering
i hope you don't push it away
i hope you pull it closer
into a warm embrace
when you feel the sadness lingering
i hope you ask it to take a seat
i hope you get to know it
and see what makes its heart beat

you are the tunnel
i see your light at the end
i will keep walking

come over tonight
and dump your heavy heart in my hands
i'll take your sorrows
and your burdens
so you can mend

how many moments have we lost to anger from
carrying burdens that weren't ours to carry

- *it's us against the world, not you against me*

even if at times we fail
to understand each other
our bodies are fluent
in the same language

your skin between my teeth
your hips between my thighs
do you mind if i stay a while?

- for old times' sake

somehow we had lost ourselves
between the setting of the sun and the rise of the moon
and we found ourselves between the sheets
like we always do
a moth to a flame
no matter how dark it gets
we always find each other's light

do you ever wonder when night falls
if we even share the same moon at all?
it feels like we're in two different worlds
we're falling apart
i wish on every shooting star,
but you're still too far.

oftentimes
i wonder if people really know
the meaning of unconditional love
you see
i love you
despite everything you did to me
i don't keep a running tally or anything
i'm just reminded sometimes
especially on the nights i can't sleep
and while i can't seem to forget
i do forgive you
and i love you
unconditionally
so much so
that i had to leave
to keep myself from ever hating you

i was empty except for fear
the fear of feeling whole
i have always been one to fear the unknown
and i feared the day i would find someone like him
because he made me feel things without being touched

i wasn't wearing rose-colored glasses
no, there was an entire garden in full-bloom
covering every inch and crevice of my mind
it was breathtaking
no one even knew there were thorns
and i was numb to the prick of them

i used to think i wasn't good enough
until you came along
and made me float
i was no longer drowning in insecurities

- *you saved me from myself*

on days i feel invisible
he finds a way to make me feel seen

i felt a promise in that kiss
and it's still lingering on my lips

i long to explore the trenches
of your mind and your heart
what a beautiful adventure it would be

you were a missing piece to my puzzle
the one i'd spent years trying to find
and you were right there the whole time
but i had to find my piece first

i didn't want to fall in love with you
but there are things in life we just can't control
no matter how hard we try
and love is one of them
i guess what i'm trying to say is
i love you
and i'd like to be with you
for however long our forever lasts
whether it's a week
a month
a year
or a hundred years
because being with you is worth the potential pain
i may have to endure if our forever falls short

i didn't have to say anything
he just knew
he enveloped me in his arms
told me it was okay to cry
as he sealed a kiss on my lips
and dried my eyes with his t-shirt

- *love is not love without all the little things*

we don't have to have it all figured out
i don't think anyway really does
as long as there's love
we're good
we have more than enough

i hold your hand
not out of habit
i hold your hand
because i never want you to think
i don't cherish every moment you're next to me

with your head upon my chest
i run my fingers through your hair
as you hum to the beat of my heart
loving you is effortless

you are my calm
and my storm
i lose myself in you
and in you i find myself too

paint your love upon my spine
stretch me
bend me
destroy me
recreate me
i want to be your masterpiece

i love the way your lips curve at the corners of your mouth
when you catch me dancing in the living room
in nothing but my underwear and your t-shirt

my body longs to be the pages of your favorite book
to feel your fingertips tracing each line
that make you pause to reread it again
because you never want to forget it

the moment he gets home
he finds her waiting for him
and he flies across the room
to get a taste of her sweet nectar

the way your fingertip
gently spells out my first name
with your last
while you're tickling my back
sets my heart to flames

i can't get enough of the way his fingertips travel
every inch of my body as if it's a map
and he's desperately in search of my treasure

you are every lyric
from my favorite songs
and even though i've memorized you
i still can't get enough of you

his tongue dances in swirls
it laps its way up and down the sides
he gently sucks and nibbles at the top
before making his way back down
he never misses a drop
i love watching as it melts against his mouth
the way he eats ice cream is truly a work of art

- *we all scream for ice cream*

his gaze drinks every inch of me
and the hunger in his eyes grows
with each subtle movement of my body
i have a hard time seeing what he sees in me
but i love my reflection in his eyes

when you think of your future
do you see yourself next to me
together hand in hand
as we walk across the street
and soak in every feeling of existence
before we're set free

in the middle of my mind
every waking thought
in the middle of my mouth
tasting your tongue
in the middle of my belly
an insatiable hunger
in the middle of my bones
deep in the marrow
in the exact middle of everything

YOU

i knew the moment i saw you
you felt like home
but not the home i'd grown used to
with no photographs on the walls
no porch with a swing
no backyard full of dandelions and peonies
no bedroom with our clothes scattered on the floor from the
night before
you felt like home
the home i've always wanted
but believed it was simply out of reach
a home with breadcrumbs sprinkled on the countertops
and coffee rings next to the kitchen sink
a home with constellations of toothpaste on the bathroom
mirrors
where the walls hold laughter
instead of echoing fears
a home with proof of memories shared
not a home full of nothing but despair
a safe space
warmth
a home i want to grow old in
i knew the moment i saw you

between these bones
i have many stories
still waiting to be told
and one day
i'll set them free from the cage in my chest
and they'll fly like birds over the sea
they'll blossom like flowers in spring
and maybe
just maybe
i'll no longer feel so heavy
and maybe
just maybe
you'll read them
and you won't feel so alone

I AM

a mother. a stepmother. a wife. a daughter. a granddaughter.
a niece. a friend. a foe. a poet or something like that. an
anxious wreck. a deep feeler. occasionally numb. a
pessimist. an optimist. impatient. a textbook definition
victim of narcissistic abuse (according to my old therapist).
not a victim. an empath. a kitchen dancer. a barefoot
walker. a singer-songwriter in another life. a whistler. a loud
belcher. socially awkward. a dreamer. a doubter. mentally
unstable in the most stable way. one in three. one in four. a
crier over almost everything (peep deep feeler and empath
above). an oversharer. a chronic overthinker. a bend until
breaker. a grudge holder. a never-ending chance giver. easily
distracted. a hyper-fixater. obnoxious. an introvert. a
procrastinator. punctual. too much. not enough. an eaves-
dropper. a people-watcher. decent at skee-ball. a spotify
listener. not a fan of microfiber cloths. a lover of stormy days
and the moon. human. okay.

ABOUT THE PUBLISHER

Harbor Lane Books, LLC is a US-based independent, digital publisher of commercial fiction, non-fiction, and poetry.

Connect with Harbor Lane Books on their website www.harborlanebooks.com and TikTok, Instagram, Facebook, Twitter, and Pinterest @harborlanebooks.